LET'S VISIT FRANCE

Let's Visit
FRANCE

BERNARD NEWMAN

BURKE

First published October 1965
Reprinted October 1967
New edition September 1971
Revised and reprinted March 1974
Third revised edition October 1978
Fourth revised edition 1983
© Bernard Newman 1965
Revisions © Burke Publishing Company Limited 1971, 1974, 1978 and 1983

ACKNOWLEDGEMENTS

The publishers are grateful to the following individuals and organisations for permission to
reproduce photographs in this book:

Air France; Pierre Allard; Anne Bolt; Commission d'Energie Atomique; The French
Government Tourist Office; The Institut Pedagogique; Paul Popper Ltd. and Geoffrey
Sherlock.

The cover photograph of the Arc de Triomphe by Gerald Clyde is reproduced by permission
of Barnaby's Picture Library.

Thanks are also due to Garry Lyle for assistance in the preparation of this edition.

ISBN   0   222   00911   X

Burke Publishing Company Ltd.,
Pegasus House, 116-120 Golden Lane, London EC1Y OTL, England.
Burke Publishing (Canada) Ltd.,
Toronto, Ontario, Canada.
Burke Publishing Company Inc.,
540 Barnum Avenue, Bridgeport, Connecticut 06608, U.S.A.
Printed in the Netherlands by Deltaprint Holland

MO 9604591

Contents

ENGLISH CHANNEL

BELGIUM

LUXEMBOURG

GERMANY

Dunkirk

Calais

Boulogne

ARTOIS

FLANDERS

PICARDY

Amiens

Bayeux

Rouen

R. SEINE

Caen

NORMANDY

ILE DE

Reims

Epernay

Paris

Versailles

FRANCE

CHAMPAGNE

LORRAINE

Nancy

Strasbourg

Troyes

R. MARNE

VOSGES

ALSACE

BRITTANY

BURGUNDY

Dijon

FRANCHE COMTE

JURA

SWITZER-LAND

R. LOIRE

CHATEAUX DE LA LOIRE

ATLANTIC

OCEAN

MARCHE

BOURBONNAIS

Lyons

LIMOUSIN

Clermont Ferrand

AUVERGNE

ALPS

SAVOY

ITALY

DAUPHINE

R. DORDOGNE

MASSIF CENTRAL

R. RHONE

Bordeaux

GUYENNE

Orange

Avignon

MONACO

R. GARONNE

LANGUEDOC

Nimes

Les Baux

PROVENCE

Grasse

Nice

GASCONY

Arles

Marseilles

PAYS BASQUE

Pau

RIVIERA

NAVARRE

Lourdes

PYRENEES

Carcassonne

SPAIN

ROUSSILLON

Llivia

ANDORRA

MEDITERRANEAN SEA

FRANCE

0   Miles   100   200

0   Km   100   200   300

CORSICA

Who Are the French?

When the Romans under Julius Caesar conquered France a little over two thousand years ago, the country was called Gaul. Its people, the Gauls, were of the Celtic race, like the Britons who then lived in what is now England and Wales. Also like the Britons, the Gauls had several centuries of Roman rule and protection, and were then left to face invasions by less civilised people. The invaders of Gaul were called Franks: hence the name France.

The Franks intermarried with the Gauls. They also took over much of the culture which the Romans had left behind them — including their language and the Christian religion. And, in time, one of their leaders brought all the tribes together as a single Frankish kingdom, with himself as the first king.

The other Frankish leaders became feudal barons — that is, they were allowed to hold and rule the lands they had taken from the Gauls, so long as they promised to accept the king as their overlord, and to provide soldiers for his army. But such promises were easily broken. So the king's power was limited. To hold it, he had to have a bigger and better army than the barons could muster.

Gradually, however, he became master of the whole of France. People began to believe in the "divine right" of kings. (The power of the king, who made all the laws, was claimed to come directly from God.) Hence the happiness of the people depended a good deal on the character of the king. If he was good, and taxes were light, the people were happy. But a bad king brought endless misery to France.

One of the king's tasks was to protect France from foreign invaders. Most of these came from Germany or Scandinavia. You will remember too that England and France were often at war, as their kings tried to seize each other's lands. From 1066 until 1558, the kings of England always held some part of France; in 1429, nearly half the country was under English rule. Then Joan of Arc, the peasant girl who became a saint, roused the French to fight against the foreigners, so that France became France again.

Yet France's troubles were not over. She suffered a series of religious wars, when Catholics fought against Protestants. True, there were also periods of splendour. Many of the French kings were named Louis, and Louis XIV was known as *le roi soleil*, the sun king. During his reign (1643-1715) France became the leading nation of Europe, and the centre of European civilisation.

It was also the centre of a large overseas empire, but the next king, Louis XV, could not hold his main overseas territories. He lost both Canada and India to the British. In his reign, too, the power of the French kings began to decline at home. New ideas were spreading across the world—

The palace of Versailles, one of the glories of France, was the home of Louis XIV

that people should rule themselves, and not be at the mercy of a man who claimed "divine right" to do as he pleased.

The French Revolution was the result. The people revolted against King Louis XVI and the nobles: thousands of aristocrats were killed. But the people did not know what to do with their new power. Their leaders, having killed the king, began to kill one another. France was in utter confusion.

Then a young military officer, named Napoleon Bonaparte, determined to restore order. This he did, and he also gained great power for himself. Eventually, in fact, he made himself emperor.

He was a great soldier, and his armies conquered many countries of Europe. But he was more than a fighter. He established the Code Napoleon—a legal system which was so good that many countries have adopted it. He built good roads which helped trade. And his soldiers carried with them some of the ideas of the Revolution—"Liberty, Equality, Fraternity" became a popular slogan.

Napoleon was overcome at last, and the French kings recovered their throne—for a while. But, by this time, the idea of the "divine right" of kings was dead. France now had a parliament.

Later, a Second Empire began, with a nephew of Napoleon as emperor. He fought a disastrous war against Germany, and lost.

Now France became a republic once more.

She was soon fighting Germany again in the First World War, which began in 1914. Her victory was dearly won— more than a million and a half Frenchmen were killed. And, in 1939, the battle with the Germans began all over again. This time France was defeated in six weeks, not to recover until the British and American victories five years later.

But the coming of peace did not mean the end of the troubles of France.

A Note on Geography

The outline of France seems simple. The country is almost square in shape, and there are few inlets and headlands, few offshore islands—and some of these, the Channel Islands, are not part of France.

France is bounded partly by land frontiers—on the east with Belgium, Luxembourg, Germany, Switzerland and Italy, and on the south with Spain—and partly by the coastline. To the north is what we call the English Channel—why "English"? the French want to know. They call it La Manche (meaning "the sleeve") because of its shape. To the south-east is the Mediterranean, whose waters wash the countries of Southern Europe, Western Asia, and Northern Africa. And to the west the Atlantic forms a seaway to the Americas. These boundaries enclose an era of about 211,000 square miles (547,000 square kilometres) and so make France the largest country in Europe, apart from Russia.

The climate is varied. That of northern France is slightly warmer than England's. That of the south, however, is much warmer. The Riviera is noted for its sunshine, and even its winters are mild, although they can be spoiled by cold winds from the mountains. These come from the north or north-west and are called the *mistral* and the *tramontane*. But they pass and the warm weather returns.

The surface of the land varies greatly—from the high Alps to the central plain. Perhaps the most important physical aspect of France is its rivers. These form some of the country's regional boundaries.

Since 1972, France has been divided into 22 regions, and each region is divided into *départements*, or counties. The smaller regions have only two or three *départements*, the larger ones from four to seven—in all there are 96. Some of the regions have the same names, and roughly the same boundaries, as the provinces into which France was divided in earlier times, and the people are glad of this. They still think fondly of the ancient provinces and it is quite common for people to refer to themselves as Bretons, Normans or Provençales.

A bridge across the River Garonne, at Toulouse. This river, along with the Dordogne, Loire, Rhone and Seine, forms some of the regional boundaries of France.

Paris

France's capital is Paris—one of the great cities of the world. With a population of over nine million, it is also one of the world's biggest cities. People have lived here for more than two thousand years, and Paris is a surprising mixture of ancient and modern. The busy streets are lined with some of the most famous shops in the world; yet just down a side street is a church a thousand years old.

The best known landmark in Paris is the Eiffel Tower. From the top there is a wonderful view of the whole city, with the River Seine wandering slowly through a maze of buildings. However, many visitors prefer to see the city from the top of a much newer landmark, a skyscraper called the Montparnasse Tower. Completed in 1973, the Montparnasse Tower is one of the many very modern buildings which have been changing the city's skyline in recent years. Among the sights which may be seen from either tower is the beautiful cathedral of Notre Dame, on an island in the River Seine. Notre Dame took hundreds of years to build. It was begun in the twelfth century, on the site of an old church, and all the inhabitants of Paris helped to dig the foundations.

Close to Notre Dame is the Sainte Chapelle—the Holy Chapel. One of the French kings who, because of his gentle character, became known as St. Louis, obtained what he

13

believed was Jesus' crown of thorns. He then built the chapel
to receive this precious relic. The Sainte Chapelle is one of
the most beautiful buildings in the world, with magnificent
stained glass windows.

Notre Dame and the Sainte Chapelle are in the oldest
part of Paris. So, too, is the Louvre which was once a palace
of the kings of France; it is now a famous art gallery and
general museum. But only a short walk away from all three
stands one of the city's newest buildings. This is the Georges
Pompidou Centre for Art and Culture, opened as recently
as 1977. The main attractions of the Centre are a great
collection of twentieth-century art and a public library

14

of more than one million books. Visitors are also offered films, plays, concerts, ballet, lectures, exhibitions and even a circus.

If the visitors are children, they may also use a special children's library, and a workshop which helps those who are interested in painting, music, sculpture and acting. For people who are just passing by, there is an attraction in the building itself. Unlike any other building in Paris—or perhaps anywhere else—the Pompidou Centre looks as though its builders have gone away and left their scaffolding

The Georges Pompidou Centre

behind them. But the framework which surrounds the outer walls is not scaffolding. It is the pipes for air-conditioning and water, and the escalators which carry people from floor to floor—designed to stand outside for a change.

At the heart of Paris lies the famous Champs Elysées. At one end of this beautiful wide avenue is the Place de la Concorde and at the other is the Etoile—the Star—where twelve streets meet.

Besides the well-known boulevards Paris has many narrow side streets. Here there are little shops and restaurants, children at play, the people of Paris going to work: shop-

The great palace of Fontainebleau, one of the largest of the royal residences of France

girls and clerks hurriedly, others taking their time. If they are walking by the River Seine, they may pass rows of open-air bookshops, and stalls where young artists try to sell their first pictures. The traffic on the streets is heavy but sometimes it is possible to escape from the noisy buses by taking a boat cruise—along the River Seine. Or, if you are in a hurry, you may travel by the "Métro"—the Paris underground railway.

There are some interesting places on the outskirts of Paris. To the south, at the edge of a forest, lies the great palace of Fontainebleau. Despite its immense size—it has more than a thousand rooms—Napoleon complained that it was impossible to find a place to be alone in it. So he built a little pavilion in the middle of the lake, and allowed no boat on it but his own—so that once he had rowed himself across no one could disturb him!

Perhaps the most interesting place of all, however, is the vast palace of Versailles. In the 17th century the great courtyard was thronged by courtiers in colourful costumes, horses and carriages, servants, dogs and horses of the king's hunt, or solemn statesmen waiting on the king for an audience.

Inside the palace is the fascinating Hall of Mirrors—in its kingly days it was lighted by 3,000 candles, each reflected a hundred times.

Just outside are the famous fountains, offering a water spectacle which cannot be surpassed anywhere in the world. The park is huge. In one corner is the Trianon—a

17

The Pont Neuf—although its name means the "New Bridge" it is actually the oldest bridge in Paris today

smaller palace where queens and their ladies used to play at being dairymaids!

There is always something fresh to see in Paris. In the suburb of Robinson you may copy the Swiss Family and have lunch up a tree. In the city itself, you can go for a boat ride on the sewers, below the streets. On a bridge across the Seine is the Statue of Liberty. You are quite right—the real Statue of Liberty is just outside the harbour of New York. But its sculptor, Bartholdi, was a Frenchman, and a copy of his famous work stands near the centre of Paris.

The Old Provinces of France

Looking out across the Channel towards Cornwall is the province of Brittany. The province is called Brittany because its people—the Bretons—are descended from the Ancient Britons who once lived in what is now England. When some of these Britons fled from the invading Anglo-Saxons, most sought safety in Wales and Cornwall, but others crossed the sea and founded Brittany. Today, Brittany is one of the 22 regions of France, but the Bretons are still noticeably different from other French people. They are similar to the Welsh, and share with the Welsh many ancient customs and legends—the stories of King Arthur and Merlin, for example.

The coastline of Brittany is broken, with many rocky inlets. There are also lovely beaches which become very popular in the summer. Inland, the country is hilly with plenty of woodland. This is not surprising since at one time the whole of Brittany was covered by a great forest. Many of the people are either farmers or fishermen.

The people of Brittany are very religious, and they are almost all Catholics. Brittany is famous for its *pardons*, or pilgrimages, some of which attract tens of thousands of people. A special service may be held to bless the fishermen's

A "pardon": Breton women, dressed in traditional costume, walk in procession to church

boats; in some villages, the people may even take their horses and cows to church to be blessed!

Most Bretons are short, thick-set, and dark-haired. There is more than a touch of superstition mingled with their Christian faith. Some Bretons are very quiet, others delight in telling tall stories; some are sociable, others seldom smile. All eat well. The Breton housewife is rarely put out if unexpected visitors arrive. She has her stock-pot, or *cautriade*, in which oddments of fish are popped as they come to hand. Potatoes are added to the fish, and they are left to cook in butter. The people are fond of salt pork, and of a smoked sausage which will keep for months before being served in hot water. The fare in Brittany is less varied than in many other French provinces, but it is very solid!

France is famous for its cooking, and every province has its own specialities. In Brittany everybody eats fish, cooked in a hundred different ways.

Many provinces—Brittany amongst them—still retain their old costumes. Once everybody used to wear them, almost as a uniform. They can still be seen at a village market, or at a *pardon* where they are often worn. The old women wear long black dresses—the young women prefer white—with a pretty head-dress of white lace.

In the language they speak the Bretons again resemble the Welsh. Some of the old people speak only Breton, which is a Celtic language akin to Welsh or Cornish. Many

A Breton girl

Bretons continue to speak this at home, but also learn French at school. Some of the younger people, in the eastern districts, speak nothing but French. Here again they resemble the Welsh, some of whom are bilingual while others do not know their own language!

Brittany is a great promontory, jutting out into the Atlantic. Its boldest headland is called Finistère—*finis terrae*, in Latin—Land's End. So far as France is concerned, this is true. Its western promontory is called Cornouaille—pronounced almost like Cornwall.

NORMANDY

To the north-east of Brittany lies the province of Normandy. It was founded by a Viking chief from Scandinavia, and soon became very powerful. One of its dukes was William the Conqueror, who became king of England in 1066, after winning the Battle of Hastings. William gave a very fine system of law to England as well as to Normandy, and we use quite a lot of his ideas today.

The Normans were famous builders, and Normandy has some beautiful cathedrals and historic castles. It is a renowned agricultural area, producing well-known breeds of horses and cows. It supplies much food to Paris, which is not too far away. Its countryside is green and pleasant, with plenty of woods.

The principal city of Normandy is Rouen, on the River Seine. It was badly damaged in the last war, but it still has its ancient and beautiful corners, and a magnificent cathe-

The cathedral of Rouen

dral. It is a great commercial centre, so famous for its textile industry that at one time all woollen and cotton goods were called *Rouenneries*.

A much smaller city which also suffered damage during the Second World War is Caen. In 1944, the British and American forces landed on the Normandy beaches and great battles raged about Caen. Not far away, however, is a little town which escaped serious damage—Bayeux. This is the home of the famous Bayeux tapestry, which is thought to have been worked by Queen Matilda, the wife of William the Conqueror, and her court ladies. The tapestry, which is a long and narrow band of linen, depicts the history of the Norman Conquest: it is a kind of history book in needlework.

The Normans are larger and stronger than the average Frenchman. They are adventurous, and are talented in business as well as in the arts. Their green land has produced excellent farmers. Nowadays, many of the young men go to the towns and become skilled workers in industry. The Normans are proud of their province, and one Norman will always help another: you could compare the Normans with members of a Scottish clan. During the French Revolution the aristocrats lost most of their land and the legal right to their titles. But the titles still survive; Normandy is the home of *six* dukes.

The Normans eat large and very tasty meals, washed down with cider. A halt is called in the middle of the meal,

A rich Normandy pasture

and Calvados—a brandy distilled from apples—is served. The halt is known as "the Norman gap".

A meal may have as its main course tripe, mussels, veal, sole, or poultry. But you may be sure of this—every Norman meal will end with one of the wonderful cheeses of the province.

PAYS DE LOIRE AND THE ILE-DE-FRANCE

South of Normandy is the valley of the Loire, not a historic province, but nonetheless a very famous region. It is especially well known for its castles.

In feudal days the barons were always fighting one another. They lived in very strongly fortified castles, where they could defend themselves against their enemies. This worked very well until someone invented gunpowder. Then the castles became almost useless, for guns could knock down their walls.

So ideas began to change. Why should rich people live in very uncomfortable castles which now offered no protection? Hence the nobles began to build chateaux, or big country houses, which were designed not as fortresses, but to be lived in.

The kings of France led the way, and their enormous palaces are among the finest of the Loire chateaux. Largest of all is Chambord, a magnificent building. You may walk through its enormous rooms by day, and you may see it floodlit at night.

Another chateau, Chenonceaux, is actually built in the

25

The chateau of Chambord with its decorative turrets

River Cher, and is very picturesque. Chambord and Chenonceaux are comparatively modern buildings, for they date back no more than four hundred years.

Amboise, which is older, is built on a hill, and has withstood sieges in its day. There is a verse in a hymn about the rich man in his castle, the poor man at his gate. At Amboise the poor man lived—and still lives—*under* the rich man's castle, in crude caves, hacked out of the limestone. The kitchen smoke finds its way out as best it can; but the caves are cool and surprisingly well furnished. And it is wonderfully quiet.

Blois, too, has an historic castle, the scene of dramatic events in French history. Chinon is now a picturesque ruin, but with what memories! It was here that Joan of Arc sought out the weak Charles VII, to persuade him to fight for his lost kingdom. At that time, the "new" chateaux had not been built; and but for her they might never have been built; France would have remained an English province.

A curious kind of building is to be seen here and there throughout the Loire valley. It is an ordinary farmhouse but it has one or two turrets at its corners, as if it were pretending to be a little castle. One farmer, indeed, called his house a "baby chateau".

To the north of the Loire lies another old province which has the peculiar title "Isle of France", although in fact it is surrounded by land, not water. In older days it was the centre of France, a royal enclosure surrounded by the lands of local barons.

A beautiful chateau reflected in the river—a familiar sight along the Loire

The Isle of France—or Ile-de-France—is not very large. In fact, one of the first kings of France used to claim that he could ride right round his domain in a single day! It still retains its name—I have heard peasants in the neighbouring province of Champagne who were about to cross the River Marne say that they were "going to France".

The Isle of France is charming rather than beautiful, but it has some fine old towns. There is Senlis, where the first king of France lived; Chantilly, with a fine chateau and a great pool filled with carp—which bite if you stick your finger in the water! There is a palace at Compiègne which is now a museum, housing among other things a transport exhibition ranging from stage-coaches to perambulators.

FLANDERS, ARTOIS AND PICARDY

In the extreme north of France is Flanders, with Artois and Picardy close by. These are prosperous regions, whose towns manufacture cloths of different kinds. Yet throughout history their plains have been a battleground. It was here that the battles of Agincourt and Crécy were fought long ago. And it was in this land of small farms that the bitterest fighting of the First World War took place—and the campaign of the Second World War which ended at Dunkirk. Every few miles there is a war cemetery; although beautifully tended, they are a frightening reminder of the terrible losses suffered in these fields. Another less tragic reminder is a small coalfield, where many of the pits are joined underground by galleries. At one time in the First World War the battle-line ran right through the middle of the coalfield. Spies used to go down one pit, along a gallery, and come up on the other side of the trench-line!

The local people are hard-working and persistent: they have so often had to rebuild their towns or villages destroyed by war.

The largest town of the region is Amiens, with a beautiful cathedral. Around the city are the *hortillonnages*—market gardens laid out among tiny canals, along which boats carry their produce to market.

The province of Picardy provided the early kings of France with many of their best regiments. The men are sturdy and intelligent, with a sense of humour—and they are still good soldiers.

CHAMPAGNE

Towards the east is Champagne; its hills are covered by vineyards which produce the famous wine. It is a land of chalk ridges, their sides planted with endless rows of vines.

The city of Reims lies within this province. Reims has a wonderful old cathedral, in which the kings of France used to be crowned. Even before that it was the ancient capital of a Gallic tribe. So was Troyes, which later became capital of the province of Champagne. (The modern capital is Châlons-sur-Marne.) Not far away is Provins. There the local product is not grapes but roses. It was the red rose of Provins which was adopted by the English house of Lancaster as its badge during the Wars of the Roses.

Wine-cellars at Reims. It is small wonder that the French name for them is *les caves*!

The province does not take its name from its famous wine —the wine takes its name from the province. Epernay is the centre of the champagne industry, and there or at Reims you may visit the vast underground galleries where the wine is stored while it matures.

Champagne has played its part in many wars. In 1914 it was invaded by the Germans. The soldiers, however, were unused to endless supplies of strong wine, and got drunk. It has been said that this helped the French and British to beat them in the Battle of the Marne!

ALSACE-LORRAINE

Still keeping eastward, we come to Lorraine. Its capital, Nancy, has one of the loveliest squares in Europe, built by a Polish king. A king of France married the daughter of King Stanislas of Poland. He later lost his kingdom, so his son-in-law made him Duke of Lorraine. Stanislas built the lovely square named after him.

Lorraine is one of the great manufacturing centres, with a flourishing iron and steel industry; the land here contains the largest iron-ore deposits in Europe and the coal needed for smelting the ore. To the east of Lorraine are the green valleys of the Vosges Mountains. On the other side of the range is Alsace, one of the loveliest provinces of France and another very important industrial area.

Alsace-Lorraine means a great deal to the French. When the Germans defeated them in 1871, France had to surrender Alsace and about a third of Lorraine. Yet the French never

31

gave up hope, and in 1918 they recovered their lost provinces.

The Alsatians—the people, not the dogs—were originally a German tribe, and Alsace has belonged to Germany and France in turn. The local dialect, freely spoken, is very like German; but in their minds the people have long been attracted by France.

Think of one incident. At the time of the French Revolution an army gathered around Strasbourg, the Alsatian capital. Before it marched off, the Mayor invited its officers to dinner one night. He turned to one young man during the meal. "Rouget, you're a musician," he said. "Why don't you write us a marching song! We ought to have one, you know."

The young man went to his room, and through the night his violin was heard. The next morning Rouget de l'Isle appeared at breakfast.

"I've got it!" he cried.

So the Mayor's daughter played the accompaniment while Rouget sang what was to become the most famous marching song in the world. Some weeks later it was adopted by the men of Marseilles, then marching to battle, and it took their name. But it should have been called the *Strasbourgaise,* not the *Marseillaise.*

At the junction of two canals with the navigable River Rhine, Strasbourg is France's main inland port as well as an important factory centre. Since 1950, it has also been the headquarters of the Council of Europe.

The storks have chosen an unlikely place to build their nest! But nests of this kind are not an unusual sight in the Vosges Mountains

Alsace is a lovely land. Picturesque villages nestle at the foot of the Vosges Mountains. Behind them the vineyards stretch up the hillsides. And every village has its family of storks. If a pair of storks nest on your chimney, you would never think of driving them away: they are supposed to bring good fortune to your home.

In Alsace almost every village has its own costume. Usually the girls wear a black skirt with a brightly-coloured bodice, and their hair is held in place by a huge bow of ribbon. The costumes are worn on a Sunday, or on a festival day when there will be folk songs and dancing.

33

Strasbourg has preserved many of its old buildings, both large and small. This one is the Chateau de Rohan

FRANCHE-COMTE

To the south of Alsace the mountains are more extensive —first the Juras and then the Alps. The Juras are in the Franche-Comté which has long been a border province, and so has seen plenty of wars. Julius Caesar found it an easy conquest because its Gallic tribes were too busy fighting each other to fight him.

Most of the Jura Mountains are gentle green hills, fine grazing grounds for flocks of sheep. Except in the towns, this is a quiet region. Its people are serious and hard-working, but they are lively enough on a festival day. Most people go to church, and then they feast! In every village an ox, some pigs and dozens of fowl are slaughtered. A traditional dish is *gaude*, a porridge made of maize and sweetened with sugar. This is eaten *after* the enormous meat course. Sausages of huge size are also popular, and so, too, are fresh fish cooked in white wine. The local cheeses are enormous; they provide the final course of the meal.

SAVOY-DAUPHINE, BURGUNDY, AND LYONNAIS

Further south is the twin-province of Savoy-Dauphiné, which borders on both Switzerland and Italy. Here the mountains are really high—in fact, they include the summit

The town of Chamonix with Mont Blanc in the background

A Burgundian vineyard

of Mont Blanc, the highest mountain in Europe. At one time
it was believed that the high valleys were the homes of
dragons and demons. Now, less romantically, they are used
for winter sports.

One of the counts of the province was Guy the Fat. He had
a dolphin painted on his coat of arms. A successor to Guy
the Fat, Humbert II, sold Savoy-Dauphiné to the king of
France. Humbert had no children, and one of the conditions
of the sale was that the eldest son of the king should always

bear a title taken from his coat of arms. So that was why the heir to the French throne was always called the Dolphin— or Dauphin in French.

Moving inland we reach the historic province of Burgundy, where dukes were at one time as powerful as the kings of France and often their enemies. During the Hundred Years' War between England and France, the Burgundians and the English were allies. It was the Burgundians who captured Joan of Arc—and sold her to the English.

Today the province is famous for its wines—and for many good things to eat—including frogs, which are considered to be a great delicacy. The countryside is green and fertile, and its old towns are very picturesque, with their ancient cathedrals and castles which have withstood many sieges in Burgundy's frequent wars.

The Burgundian vineyards are often amazingly small. Clos-Vougeot, for example, is a world-famous wine, but its grapes are grown in an area of only 125 acres (50·5 hectares).

At Beaune there is a lovely old medieval hospital, still in use. An annual wine-tasting ceremony is held here, followed by an auction of local wines. It is this auction which governs the prices for the rest of the Burgundy vintage.

In earlier times, Burgundy contained the old city of Lyons, but in 1312 King Philippe IV took the territories around it for himself, and it became the capital of its own province, Lyonnais. More recently, it has become the capital of a newly-formed region called Rhone-Alpes, which takes in several of the ancient provinces—including Savoy-Dauphiné.

Once famous for its silk industry, Lyons is now better known for making synthetics like nylon, as well as cars, machinery and chemicals. These industries, and also the whole of south-western France, take their electricity supply from several new hydro-electricity stations on the Rhone.

Lyons' fast-growing population of over one million makes it the second city in France, and as it cannot comfortably hold so many people a completely new city is being built at l'Isle d'Abeau, about 20 miles (32 kilometres) to the south. This will gradually provide housing and work for 200,000 people who would otherwise make Lyons even more crowded.

PROVENCE

Moving southwards towards the Mediterranean one comes to Provence, and to the ancient town of Orange (which has nothing to do with fruit). It was once a famous Roman city, and it has a Roman theatre which is still in use after 2,000 years. Very much later, one of its counts passed on his title to the house of Nassau—the family of the English King William III and of the Dutch royal family, who are still known as the House of Orange.

Still further south is another interesting town, Avignon. In the fourteenth century there was a great religious quarrel between two Popes, both reigning at the same time—one lived in Rome, the other in Avignon. The Palace of the Popes still stands in Avignon, overlooking the town and the Rhone valley.

The
St. Benezet
Bridge—only
four arches
remain of the
original
fifteen

There is a famous French nursery rhyme about the bridge at Avignon:

> *"Sous le pont d'Avignon*
> *On y danse, on y danse."*

This is the broken bridge of St. Benezet. Some people sing *sur*—*on* the bridge—but *sous*, or under, is correct, for one arch of the bridge is astride the road and beneath it is a favourite place for children to play. Another arch, now vanished, used to straddle an island in the middle of the river.

Not far from Avignon is the mountain stronghold of Les

The heart of Roman France: Arles, with the amphitheatre (right)

Baux. According to legend, its lords were descended from Balthasar (one of the Three Wise Men) and their device was the star of Bethlehem. Now the little town is just a heap of ruins, set in a commanding situation. Yet Les Baux is still of significance, for in the last century beds of aluminium ore were discovered near by. The ore was called *bauxite*, after the ruined town.

Provence used to be the home of the romantic troubadours, who went from castle to castle singing their lays, which were composed on the spot, perhaps about the beauty of some local lady.

It was the first region of Gaul to be occupied by the Romans, and it is still known as "Roman France". Here

there are some famous Roman remains. The great amphi-
theatres at Arles and Nimes are actually still used for concerts, or for Provencal bullfights. These are bullfights with a
difference: the bull is not killed or seriously hurt. It enters
the ring with a rosette fastened between its horns, and
dozens of young men rush around trying to snatch the
rosette off. This can be dangerous, however, for the bulls are
agile and often get angry. In addition there are other fights
between terrible enemies. At Arles there was once a fight in
the arena between a bull and a tiger—and it was the tiger
which turned and ran for its life!

One of the kings of Provence had an interesting connec-
tion with England. This was King René, whose court was

A moment of danger at a Provencal bullfight

so gay and lively. One of his daughters, Margaret, married Henry VI of England, and played a courageous part in the Wars of the Roses. René himself was a famous troubadour; he also wrote verses and painted pictures.

In the east, Provence is very mountainous, but towards the coast the country gradually softens, and the mountains become gentle hills. Among these hills is the little town of Grasse, which is noted for its scent factories.

The professional wine-taster is a very important person in the French vineyard districts. These men have an unusual gift of taste which enables them to judge the quality of the wines. Similarly, at Grasse are men called "noses" or samplers. Their job is to sniff at the essences, to judge *their* quality. The men claim that their trade cannot be learned, but the skill is passed on from father to son. In Grasse, the scent of the lavender is so strong that it affects the local corn, and can be tasted in the bread!

From Grasse it is not far to the Mediterranean, one of the playgrounds of Europe, with a beautiful coast and warm climate. Here are such famous resorts as Nice (which is also a large industrial city) and Cannes. Further along the coast is Monte Carlo, which is not in France at all but is part of the independent principality of Monaco. The people of Monaco, called Monégasques, are not subject to the French laws and do not pay French taxes. They are ruled by a council headed by Prince Rainier—whose princess was, before her marriage, the film star Grace Kelly. There are gambling casinos at all French resorts, but that of Monte

Carlo is the most famous, and draws visitors from all over the world.

Of course, not everybody goes to the Riviera to gamble. Most of its visitors are in search of the sun, and they are seldom disappointed. An attractive custom during local festivals is to hold a Battle of Flowers. Here the carnival floats (lorries) carry scenes made up entirely of flowers; pretty girls ride along on them; music and dancing follow, with the people throwing flowers at each other. These are always very lively and light-hearted affairs.

The town and harbour of Monte Carlo

The Battle of Flowers at Nice

LANGUEDOC AND BOUCHES DU RHONE

In the west, Provence joins the old province of Languedoc, and here the River Rhone forms a great delta on its way to the sea. But first, one tributary passes under the Pont du Gard—one of the finest Roman monuments in the world. This is a great aqueduct, consisting of three tiers of arches, built to carry the waters of the River Eure to the Roman city of Nimes. It is no longer used as an aqueduct, but its lower course still serves as a bridge.

44

The Rhone delta area is called Bouches du Rhone (Rhone Mouths), but the land within the delta is known as the Camargue. This land has been formed by the great volume of silt which the Rhone carries—and is still carrying—down from the mountains.

Here, wide marshes make a home for many wild birds, especially the beautiful pink and white flamingoes. And on the higher ground there are vineyards, ricefields, sugar plantations and ranches on which wild horses roam.

There are also some interesting towns—for instance, Aigues-Mortes (Dead Waters) which was built as a seaport but is now three miles (about five kilometres) inland, and Les Saintes-Maries-de-la-Mer, which is still on the sea.

Les Saintes-Maries is named after St. Mary Magdalen, and two of the other Marys who were followers of Jesus.

**The Roman aqueduct
north-east of Nimes**

According to a legend, these three Marys fled from the Holy Land to the Camargue after Jesus was crucified, bringing with them a black servant girl named Sarah. Sarah became the patron saint of gypsies, and in May each year gypsies from all over Europe gather at Les Saintes-Maries for a festival in her honour. During the festival, they take her statue from the church, and carry it into the sea.

East of Les Saintes-Maries, and outside the Camargue, stand two of France's most important cities. They are Toulon, a naval base and shipbuilding centre, and Marseilles, the capital of the Bouches du Rhone *département*. Marseilles is France's main seaport, and third largest city. Though not on the River Rhone, it is linked with the river by a canal, and as the Rhone has canal links with rivers flowing north-

Wild horses of the Camargue. They are small but strong, and world-famous for their beauty

A view from
the church of
the town of
Les Saintes-
Maries

ward it is possible to travel by inland waterways right through France, and also from France through Germany and Holland.

These waterways are much used by cargo barges, and so too is the Canal du Midi, which from the coast of Languedoc links the Mediterranean Sea with the Atlantic Ocean. On this canal is the large industrial city of Toulouse, which is the main centre for making the popular European Airbus illustrated on page 78.

The name Languedoc was originally spelt Langue d'oc, which means "language of oc". The language spoken in Languedoc and neighbouring southern provinces used to be quite different from that of northern France. In the south, the word for "yes" was *oc*; in the centre and north it was *oil*—now changed into *oui*. So the two divisions of

47

France were distinguished by the difference in their word for "yes"—*Langue d'oc* and *Langue d'oil*.

ROUSSILLON AND ANDORRA

The old language of Provence is still spoken in the next province, Roussillon, although it has borrowed freely from Catalan. Its people are Catalans, and they are scattered across the eastern end of the Pyrenees—there are far more of them in Spain, around Barcelona, than in France. Catalonia used to be an independent kingdom, including the island of Majorca, and the palace of its kings still stands in Perpignan.

Away to the north is a famous city called Carcassonne. This is a medieval fortress, restored to all its ancient grandeur—ramparts, battlements, baileys, towers—every historic excitement you could imagine.

There are two rather curious facts connected with this region. The first is associated with a little place called Llivia. In 1659 France gained a victory over Spain, and by the peace treaty Spain had to yield the valley and villages of the Upper Cerdagne. But Llivia protested—it was not, it claimed, a village, but a town—and legally it actually was. So it remained, and still forms, part of Spain, connected to its motherland by a neutral road across a corner of France.

Not far away is a tiny country—not merely a town, but a whole country—which belongs neither to France nor to Spain. When the Frankish Emperor Charlemagne and his sons drove the Moors out of France, they established a num-

A remote and lonely-looking region in the Pyrenees

ber of settlements in the valleys of the Pyrenees. Here
soldiers were given grants of land: in return they were to
act as outposts against the Moors, who were still the
masters of Spain. And so, along the Pyrenees, a chain of
tiny republics was formed, each with a local baron as its
overlord.

As the Moors were driven further south, however, the
local barons seized these territories. But one of them escaped
because of a lucky accident: the lawyers who drew up the
charter for Andorra gave it two overlords instead of one—
the Count of Urgel and the Prince-Bishop of Urgel—and

neither would admit the other's claim. Eventually they agreed to share their rights.

So, today, Andorra is still an independent republic. The Bishop of Urgel is still one of its overlords; the other is the President of France, who has taken over the rights of the Count.

The Andorrans are a Catalan people. Their little country, which is about the size of the Isle of Wight and has a population of 30,000, is ruled by a Council and a President. The people are quite prosperous. At one time they used to live by smuggling goods from France into Spain, or vice versa! Now, however, hundreds of French and others visit Andorra as a holiday centre. The country is entirely mountainous, and is very attractive. One of the most successful escape routes of the Second World War ended in Andorra. It was to this tiny land across the Pyrenees that prisoners-of-war escaped and shot-down airmen were smuggled from German-occupied France.

NAVARRE; THE BASQUES

Near the western end of the Pyrenees is Navarre. One of its most famous towns is Lourdes, with its pilgrimage shrine. Here, a hundred years ago, a peasant girl saw a holy vision. Thereafter miracles were reported—and are still credited in our own day.

Not far away is Pau which was once the capital of Navarre—and the home of Henry, a famous local king who finally acquired the crown of France. His province of

Basque dancers performing one of their traditional dances

Navarre was prosperous; his aim was that the humblest peasant had "a fowl in the pot" every Sunday.

Only about one-tenth of Navarre is on the northern side of the Pyrenees; most of it is in Spain. It was once part of the territory of the Vascones—or Basques and Gascons. A legend claims that these people were descended from Japhet, son of Noah, who settled in Navarre after the Flood. Navarre first appears in written history as an independent kingdom in the seventh century.

The Basques are a people apart—different not merely from the French, but from every other people of Europe. Their language is quite distinct from all others, and is very difficult to learn. It is called Eskuanaldac—and that is just about the easiest word in it. The Basques are a very well-behaved people. Their explanation is that the Devil tried to

51

A game of pelota in full swing

learn their language, but failed, and so was unable to tempt
them!

They have a rich culture of their own. It includes local
ballets, with gay dancing; hobby-horse dances, and sword
dances. These are very athletic—with much leaping into the
air and mad twirling. The costumes worn by men and
women alike are gay and colourful, and include one item
that has become world-popular—the Basque beret.

Their game, pelota, has also spread around the world. A
hard ball is hit by a wicker claw fastened to the arm, and
banged against a concrete *fronton* (wall) with great force.
If no *fronton* is available, the small boys often play pelota

52

up against a church wall or any other convenient and high wall.

The Basques cling firmly to their ancient ties. It is quite usual to find a farm which has been worked by the same family for hundreds of years. Some Basques go to South America to make their fortune—but they always return to their own land. Again, four-fifths of the Basques live on the Spanish side of the Pyrenees.

AQUITAINE

Our survey of the old provinces of France is not yet quite finished. Aquitaine was once part of the domains of the English crown—it was given as part of the dowry of Eleanor of Aquitaine when she married Henry II. At that time the duchy extended from the River Loire to the Pyrenees, and included the counties of Gascony and Guyenne.

Bordeaux is the capital of this region. And it has the air of a capital: more than once, in fact, it has served as the capital of France. It is of course a great port for a large and prosperous district. Its buildings range from the Roman to the very modern. And it is not ashamed of its long association with England, when it was the chief town of Aquitaine, belonging to the English kings.

LIMOUSIN, MARCHE, AUVERGNE, AND BOURBONNAIS

Inland again lie the little-known regions of Limousin and Marche. Here, the most interesting town is Limoges, famous

53

Sheep grazing on poor pasture in Auvergne

for its porcelain and enamel ware. Round it is a district of heathland and forests.

Next is Auvergne—the "Central Massif"—often called "the roof of France". True, its mountains are not nearly as high as the Alps, but they are the source of many great rivers. This is the land of the *causses*, high tablelands separated by deep ravines. The soil is thin here, and peasants scrape its surface to form a *sotch*—a small patch of land in which things will grow. The north is mostly cattle-rearing country; the south sheep-farming. But everywhere conditions are tough. However, there are plans to improve both the water supply and the condition of the soil.

"Lack of water is our difficulty," said a shepherd. "Though

our sheep have learned to do without it. They can go for long periods without drinking—like camels."

It is little wonder that the population of Auvergne is decreasing; and in fact whole villages have been abandoned and are falling into ruins. The Auvergnats are a sturdy people, but they find life too hard and its rewards too small —especially when compared with the attractions of the towns.

Such towns as there are in southern Auvergne are interesting, and most of their industries are based on local products. Millau makes fine gloves of lambskin, soft and supple. Near by is Roquefort, where a famous cheese is made from ewes' milk. The local people are very practical— Rodez has a lovely cathedral, and a television company has a relay station on its roof!

Moving northwards, one passes from sheep to cattle

The vaults at Roquefort where the cheeses are stored

country. The cows live in barns during the winter, and each village has its own fixed date for releasing them. Every year they are herded up on to the mountainsides to graze on the Spring grass. The men who accompany each herd stay with it for the summer. They live in a *buron*, a stone hut, which also serves as a dairy.

And they cheat the cows. Most of these have calves, and will refuse to yield milk to the cowmen in order to feed their young. So when a calf runs to its mother, a herdsman will tie it to a front leg of the cow, and then proceed to milk her. The cow, feeling her calf close at hand, thinks that she is feeding him! The calf does get a drink, however, but not until the man has enough milk in his pail.

The mountains and tablelands, because they are almost deserted, were used by the French Resistance Movement during the last war in their fight to free their country from the Germans. Here arms were dropped and agents were landed by parachute. The men—and women—of the Resistance harassed the Germans, but suffered in return.

In the villages the old costumes are still worn. The women wear long dresses, with white lace blouses and coloured shawls. The men seem drab in comparison, though their dark suits are enlivened by fancy waistcoats.

At the local festivals, music is supplied by a kind of bag-pipe, called a *cabrette*. The piper does not blow, as in Scotland—he sings at the same time as he plays. So he presses the bellows with his elbow against his waist. The sound is quite Scottish, minus the drones.

Auvergne was once a volcanic region, and the evidence of this can still be seen. The town of Le Puy is especially interesting. It is built around the hard cones of three volcanoes! From the Puy-de-Dôme, near Clermont-Ferrand, one can see more than sixty extinct volcanoes on the skyline. And sometimes whole stretches of land are covered by great lumps of lava.

Around the Puy de Dôme there are many mineral springs, and from these is bottled much of the mineral water which French people are so fond of drinking. Puy de Dôme and the neighbouring area of Vichy supply them with about 3,000,000,000 bottles every year—and that is only one third of the amount that they drink. Clermont-Ferrand, with about 250,000 people, is the only large city in Auvergne. It has grown mainly because it is the headquarters of the great Michelin rubber company, which supplies France—and the world—with a popular brand of motor tyre, much rubber clothing, and some very good guide books. The city's factories also make machinery and chemicals, and process much of Auvergne's farm produce. Many of the factory workers are drawn from the country people who find too little reward in farming the more arid parts of the region.

To the south of Auvergne are the Cevennes Mountains; to the north, the Bourbonnais—the home of the Bourbon family, which provided France with so many kings.

It is also the home of a famous breed of cattle, the Charollais. This breed is famous for the quality of its beef, and Charollais bulls have recently been exported to Britain to improve the quality of the herds. The white Charollais cows are not particularly good milkers, but their meat is superb.

Bourbonnais was a very small province. When the old province of Auvergne became the new region of Auvergne, Bourbonnais was added to it. It is mainly a farming and mineral water area, and even its bigger towns are relatively small. The best-known of them is Vichy, the health resort to which the French government moved when the Germans invaded France in the Second World War.

CORSICA

We have not included *all* the historic provinces in our visit, for some are very like their neighbours. But there is one that we must not miss: Corsica, one of the most beautiful islands in Europe.

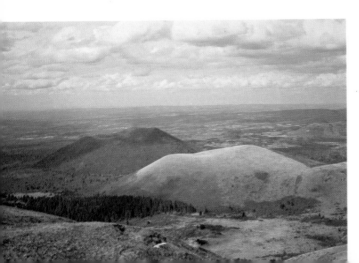

Extinct volcanoes in the Puy de Dôme area

**Calvi,
a typical
Corsican town**

It lies off the Riviera Mediterranean coast. Corsica is mainly mountainous, and quite small: a mere hundred miles (161 kilometres) long and less than 3,400 square miles (8,800 square kilometres) in area; its highest peak, Mt. Cinto, reaches 8,891 feet (2,711 metres).

Corsica is especially lovely in Spring. Then the hillsides are covered with the *maquis*, flowering shrubs, whose scent can be detected far out to sea.

Down the island's west coast are beautiful bays, and inland there are splendid forests. You will often see the timber-stacks of charcoal burners. The soil is so poor that very few crops can be raised. Indeed, many of the people make their flour from horse chestnuts.

Although the Corsicans have lived under French rule for only 200 years and come mostly of Italian stock, they are patriotic Frenchmen. One of France's greatest figures—Napoleon—was a Corsican, and thousands of his fellow countrymen followed him to the wars. Since then, tens of thousands more have emigrated to France to find work or better opportunities than they can find at home.

Some of the Corsican resorts have now become very popular. But there are plenty of villages which rarely see a visitor. Here you will meet the real Corsicans, tough and sturdy—women as well as men—with bright, lively children. Family ties are especially close, and the word of the head of the family is law. The people of Corsica are proud and independent, but kindly and friendly. They do not live richly. If they eat mutton, it is usually goat! Roast blackbirds on toast are a real delicacy! And the Corsican seas produce huge, delicious lobsters. But in any cottage they will offer you anything they have: you could not ask for more.

France Makes Good after the War

We have seen who the French are, and something of the geography of France. Now we must see how the country is governed, how its people live and earn their living. And we should begin with France's recovery from two world wars.

During both the First and the Second World Wars France was occupied by Germany. Each time, in addition to terrible

The post-war recovery of France emerges clearly in scenes such as this one: a great dam in the course of construction in Brittany

casualties, much damage was done to the country. At the end of the Second World War in 1945, a million and a half houses had been destroyed, and there was hardly a bridge left intact.

France's recovery was quite remarkable, and has been outstanding in her history. Britain also had tremendous damage to make good. The people said to the government: "We must have new houses!" and thousands of men were put to work on this task. But the French decided that houses must wait. First, the damaged factories, power plants and communications must be restored.

Even the friends of France were astonished at her progress. Within a year French industrial output was back to pre-war standards, and soon it had doubled.

Great dams were built, to harness the power of mighty rivers. The production of electricity more than trebled. New factories were constructed, with up-to-date machinery. The French railways had been backward, but now became the best and fastest in the world. In addition, oil was discovered in Algeria which was then a French colony and brought new wealth to the economy, helping the French in their drive for better conditions.

Social Services

Gradually the whole outlook of the country changed. People became confident that they could give their children a good standard of life.

They were helped by the State in the different social services. Family allowances, for example, now far exceed those paid in Great Britain. This means that a large family is no longer a heavy financial burden. The family allowances, added to a man's wages, assure a reasonable living standard.

The French medical services are somewhat similar to the British, but the French claim that they are better. A sick Frenchman pays up to thirty per cent. of his medical costs—but he can choose his hospital and surgeon. In Britain, you can go to your local hospital and have an operation free of charge. But if you wish to go into a private ward and to engage the Queen's surgeon, the operation would cost a very large sum.

Old age and other pensions are generous in France, averaging about 40% of a man's wages.

But who pays for all these benefits? The "State" is merely the people of a country. The money which it has comes from the taxes and other contributions paid by the people.

However, a wage-earner himself pays only a small part of his contribution. His employer must pay the rest, and also make some other payments on behalf of his employees. In all, more than 40% of his wage bill goes to social services.

Politics in France

The French Trades Unions are divided into three main organizations—one controlled by Communists, one by Socialists, the third by Catholics. Each has members in all the different trades. These varying loyalties tend to create a lack of unity amongst the Unions; sometimes they will agree on a claim, sometimes not.

France is a democracy—and there was a time when it seemed to be rather *too* democratic, because it had so many political parties. At parliamentary elections in most democratic countries there is usually a choice of candidates from three or four different parties, but in pre-war France there were often nine or ten—and once there were as many as fifty-two.

This meant that no party could ever win a clear majority of seats. So a group of parties would form a coalition, and try working together. But after a few months a dispute would break them up; then another group of parties would try to form a government. The result was that over a period of about eighty years the average life of a French government was about eight months—and eight months is not long enough to get much done.

After the war, the political parties again began to fight bitterly among themselves, and at the same time the vast French ·empire began to crumble. Indo-China and North Africa were lost. Then General de Gaulle took charge of the country, and a new era of prosperity began.

**Charles
de Gaulle**

Charles de Gaulle

When war broke out in 1939 General Charles de Gaulle was almost unknown in France; but when his country collapsed a year later he came to England and decided to fight on. Before the war ended he commanded a large army, to say nothing of the thousands of French people who fought the Germans in the "Resistance".

De Gaulle was not a politician but at the end of the war he became head of the Provisional Government. He hoped that Frenchmen would remain united after the war was won, but the politicians began to quarrel, and so he resigned. He was quite sure that France would need him again and would send for him, but he did not expect to wait for so long. Not until 1958 did the call come.

Then France was in trouble in Algeria, a region of North Africa which the French had ruled for nearly a hundred years, and where they had done much good for the Algerians. But in these days people like to rule themselves, and so many of the Algerians began to fight for independence. The French tired of the war, and de Gaulle saw that it could never be won. So he made peace with the rebels, on such generous terms that the French and Algerians could be friends.

Charles de Gaulle had an imposing appearance. He was also a very determined and obstinate man. As President of France he had one main aim—to make France the greatest nation in Europe.

In his efforts to make France the leader of Europe, he withdrew France from NATO (the North Atlantic Treaty Organisation), gave orders that France was to have her own nuclear weapons, and tried to make the five other members of the European Economic Community (the "Common Market") do as he wished.

The E.E.C. had been formed in 1957 by Italy, West Germany, Luxembourg, Belgium, Holland and France. At the time, Britain refused to join, but when she did apply for membership, in 1961, de Gaulle would not agree. As one of the six countries could veto anything the other five wished to do, Britain was refused admission.

There were several reasons behind de Gaulle's attitude towards Britain. He did not care much for the British; he believed they ought to have joined the Common Market at the beginning instead of waiting until it had proved a success; and he disliked Britain's friendship with America.

One effect of trying to make France the leader of Europe was actually to separate her from most of her former friends, who did not like de Gaulle's high-handed methods. De Gaulle also did little to improve the standard of living of the French workers, and gradually feelings began to rise against him. In 1968 there were very serious strikes and students and workers joined in demonstrations against de Gaulle. Once again the streets of Paris became the scene of ugly riots.

De Gaulle promised to meet a number of the demands made

by the workers. But the slowness with which this was done angered them.

One of the changes de Gaulle wished to make was to abolish the Senate, the Upper House of the French parliament. There was much opposition to this and de Gaulle decided that all the voters of France should vote on it in a referendum. Before the voting, he told Frenchmen that if they did not support his proposal, he would resign.

They did not give him their support, and de Gaulle resigned.

In the election that followed, de Gaulle's former Prime Minister, Georges Pompidou, was elected President. All France's friends hoped that this change would bring about better relationships with other countries. This did happen to a certain extent, as can be seen from the fact that Britain is now a member of the E.E.C. And international relations continued to improve under President Giscard d'Estaing, President Pompidou's successor. However, France's attitude to NATO and nuclear weapons did not change. Nor did it take much notice of outside opinions on some other matters of outside interest. De Gaulle's determination to make France the greatest nation in Europe still seemed to have its influence on French politics.

Whether it will continue to do so under the latest President, François Mitterand, has yet to be seen. President Mitterand is a socialist, with policies very different from those of de Gaulle and his successors, but it is still too early in his seven-year term of office for us to judge where those policies might lead.

How France is Governed

The head of the state is the President, with the Prime Minister and the government under him. There are two houses of parliament: the National Assembly and the Senate, as well as councils for each region, each *département* and each of the 38,000 *communes* into which the *départements* are divided.

The basis of French life is the *commune*, now officially called the *municipalité*. They range from large cities to small villages—in fact, about 24,000 of them have less than 500 inhabitants. Each *commune* has its own *Maire* (or Mayor), who is the officer of its people and at the same time the government representative. On official occasions he wears a sash of the national colours: red, white and blue.

His office, the *Mairie,* may be open every day or only two afternoons a week, according to the amount of business. The Mayor signs forms, and gives permission for this and that. He has a council, a secretary, and a *garde champêtre.* The latter is officially a village constable, but in practice he is a man of all work. In addition to his duties as a policeman, he runs errands for the Mayor, sticks up posters, and acts as town-crier. Where the council cannot afford a uniform for him, he will wear a peaked cap with an old suit.

If there is a real crime in the village, the constable sends

69

for the *gendarmes*. These are part of a national force, and are stationed in the country towns—each station may have a sergeant and half a dozen men. The gendarmes can also be called up as army reservists in case of riots. They usually "pound their beats" on bicycles. The larger towns have municipal police, whose duties are confined to their own towns.

A smaller town will have one *agent de police*—who can call upon the *gendarmerie* for reinforcements when necessary. In Paris there is the Garde Republicain, a semi-military organization.

The French people may be of different races, and some speak other languages—as well as their own, of course—but they are proud to be French. They may differ in religion, race, habits and politics, but they are all French.

In England people have faith in parliament; in France there is not the same confidence—as we have seen, governments have changed too often for that. But France still goes on, because of its Civil Service.

The head of each *département,* or county, is the *préfet.* He is the representative of the government for all purposes. And, if the government is defeated, he carries on. He cannot make new laws, of course, but until a new government is formed he governs under the old ones. The citizens will scarcely notice the difference, and the fact that someone is in charge gives them confidence.

What Sort of People Are the French?

The French are very patriotic, but they are also very thrifty. When France is in danger they will fight for her, but even for her they will not pay taxes if they can avoid them. Income tax is perhaps the fairest means of collecting revenue, but in France it is a failure as so few of the people seem to have any income! So a government, to raise the money it needs, has to impose indirect taxation—by taxing most of the things that people buy. Then not even clever people can avoid paying.

As a nation, they love to talk. You can hear endless discussions in the outdoor cafés. You might think that the men are making speeches, or even quarrelling, when in fact they are having a friendly argument, with everyone holding firmly to his opinions.

The French are a very cultured people. If a new painting arrives at a local art gallery, crowds will go to see it. Music and books are taken very seriously.

The Louvre in Paris—the most famous art museum in the world. The French people are justly proud of it

Food and Markets

By European standards, France is a big country for its population of 54,000,000, and it has large areas of very good farmland. So it can feed itself, while other countries often have to import large quantities of food, much of it in tins.

The French are very enterprising in what they eat. It is

The French take their food very seriously as can be seen from this picture!

not merely the expensive restaurants which serve a delightful meal. There are countless little eating houses which are excellent—usually the woman looks after the till, while her husband does the cooking. And even the humblest workman eats better than his English counterpart, simply because the French take far more trouble in preparing their food.

Breakfast is simple: usually fresh rolls, with coffee; no bacon or eggs. But it is surprisingly filling. Sometimes the French take "elevenses"—which to them means a glass of wine and a biscuit—but lunch is the important meal of the day. There will be soup, prepared with great care; then a dish of green vegetables, served separately. Next follows the main course—occasionally roast beef, but more often some other meat delicately stewed or braised, always with a sauce. The French are also artists in the use of offal, such as liver and kidneys. Potatoes and bread accompany the main dish, often with a bowl of salad. Then a variety of cheeses is available, with bread. Wine will be sipped between the courses. In France, wine is not a luxury drink; the ordinary local wines are very cheap and often very good.

Dinner in France follows the same pattern as lunch, but in the poorer homes the meat course is omitted.

If you want to know how seriously the French take their meals, think of the visit of King Louis XIV to Chantilly—when his host's chef committed suicide in shame because the fish was late!

Let us visit a small town on market day. Vans and carts have been driving in from the farms since before dawn. Now the old

73

women are squatting on benches, offering eggs and butter for sale. The younger women cannot be spared for the job—they are needed on the farm. There is a little whispering as the grandmas sit down; this is to decide the price of eggs for the day. And now the early housewives have arrived, to get the best food. It is not a light task; it demands serious thought.

Here are the stalls of the market gardeners, loaded with vegetables. They look very attractive—potatoes and carrots are scrubbed clean before they appear on the stalls.

Close by are the stalls of the butchers. No frozen meat from a wholesaler for them; they have chosen their animals on nearby farms. Many of the joints are small, just sufficient for the day. The butcher may shout his sales-talk, but the house-wife knows as much about meat as he does, and he knows it.

And here is another section of the market, devoted to drapers' and ironmongers' stalls. These people do not "belong". They are from a neighbouring town, and they drive around to the little markets.

Privacy is hardly possible. If a woman is buying under-wear, she cannot try it on, but holds it up against herself to see whether it fits. A man sits on the steps of a house to try on a pair of shoes.

Elsewhere there is more important business—a farmer is selling a horse. It may take some weeks, as the customer tries to bring the price down. At last he does so; the farmer, too, is satisfied, for he had already added to his price so as to be able to take "something off".

Market stalls at Aigues Mortes. The walls behind them date from the thirteenth century

The town-crier comes around, ringing his bell and making his announcements. Two men arrive with brushes, shovels and wheelbarrows: they have to clear up the mess when everybody has gone. By midday the market is over. The farmers have driven their carts away; the traders are counting up their cash and packing their goods into cases; and in a hundred homes housewives are cooking the food they have just bought.

The Farm and the Village

As might be expected, the French village depends largely on farming.

Most of the farmhouses are actually inside the village. There is nothing uniform about the buildings—they come in all kinds of sizes and shapes, and may be grouped around the village green—which is often brown!

At one side of the open space is the church; then a café, which is the social centre of the village; next the *mairie,* or town hall. A petrol pump and a few shops complete the village.

There is a bus-service to the nearest town one day a week —usually on market day. If the village is large, it will have a *salle des fêtes,* a village hall. Here a dance is held at the week-end, and maybe a cinema show one other evening. And, of course, there is a school.

The shops are very simple. Once or twice a week a butcher and baker drive in their vans and open shop for two hours.

There is no hurry in a French village. Things do not change quickly. Clothing—especially men's—is simple and usually old; it is often difficult to tell the difference between a farmer and his hired labourer.

More of the villages are still behind the times—for

example, many have no running water, but depend upon wells in back gardens. Until recently, farms were not highly mechanized and farming methods were often somewhat primitive. A tractor was a rare sight indeed. Now, however, there are nearly as many tractors as there are farms.

Crops vary, of course, according to the district—corn and sugar beet in the north, grapes in the central regions, and olives, lemons and other fruit in the south. The price of grain is fixed by the Government and is the same whether it is delivered to a co-operative or a merchant.

In some parts of the country the young people tend to drift to the towns, and farms are short of labour. Yet agriculture is still the most important industry of France.

While French farms are very mechanised today, some old customs remain. Cows are still milked by hand, in the fields, on this farm in Normandy

Industry

French factories adopted modern methods much more quickly than French farms. French aircraft are as world-famous as French motor-cars. France produces large quantities of iron, steel and other metals as well as machinery, woollen, cotton, silk and synthetic cloth, chemicals and paper. She also builds ships and railways, and dams for production of electricity. The country is, in fact, very self-contained.

Experts say that France has a "balanced" economy—a nice mixture of agriculture and industry. It may not lead to

The Airbus A300, built in France in co-operation with other E.E.C. countries. These aircraft operate between France and North Africa and each one carries a maximum of 251 passengers.

The atomic energy centre at Marcoule, in the vineyard area north of Avignon. With her current rate of industrial growth France makes good use of such atomic power stations

great wealth, but it is certainly better for the country and the people in days when trade is slack.

Women enjoy equal rights with men, including equal pay for equal work. They also play a part in French politics.

79

Schools

French educational standards are extremely high. Children have to work very hard—especially those in secondary schools. Apart from a long school day, older children bring a great deal of work home. Their parents have to sign their homework as a proof that the children have done it themselves! All children from six to sixteen years of age must go to school.

The schools do much to encourage sports. They also arrange "Vacation Camps" which are very popular. Many

A geography lesson in progress in a small, overcrowded village school

A modern secondary school

of these are just holiday centres, but older children often do some kind of public work in the camps—while having plenty of time for their own pleasures.

Unlike town schools, the village schools are inadequate

and old-fashioned. You are quite likely to find one or two teachers with 40 or 50 children of all ages. Nowadays more and more children are being taken to central schools by bus, although this is not so easy in France, where the villages are fairly widely scattered.

In France, Church and State are firmly separated, and scripture is not taught in schools. The village priest, however, holds some voluntary classes on a Thursday.

Why Thursday? Most French schools are not closed for the week-end, as it is thought better for the children to have a free day twice a week. So they go to school from Monday to Wednesday, and then on Friday and Saturday. Thursday is a holiday, except for the priest's classes and for homework.

The summer holidays are long—from the middle of July to the end of September—so that children can help on the farms during the harvest. You may often see a very small boy or girl in charge of the family cow. It will have a light rope tied to its horns, and its guardian will direct it to the best grass.

Sports and Games

When I was sixteen, I went to France with a boys' football team. The Soccer game had been introduced into France not long before, and we were to play local schools. We were warned that they were not yet very good, but to encourage them we were to let them score a goal in every match. So if the ball trickled towards our goal, our goalkeeper would

Tobogganing, a popular winter sport where there is sufficient snow

The Tour de France

fall over himself and let it go into the net. *We* usually scored ten or twelve.

Things are different today. French teams can compete with the world's best. This applies also to Rugger. Generally, Soccer is more popular in the north, Rugger in the south. Almost every village has its football field. The French are rather excitable players, but very fast.

Basket-ball is also popular, and is played with great enthusiasm. But on the whole the French are happier acting as individuals than as part of a team. They are very good at tennis, for example. But they do not play cricket, which they think is too slow.

The favourite of all French sports is cycle racing—usually over long distances. Every town has its club, and on any summer Sunday a rural road will be disturbed by a loud-speaker in a car: "Look out! The cycle race is coming!" A few minutes later the road is filled with cycles, pedalled by young men in gaily-coloured singlets and shorts.

The best of the riders compete in the Tour de France, which takes place in July. Day after day dozens of cyclists ride about France, along valleys and over mountain passes. Altogether hundreds of thousands of people watch them—

A novel form of beach sport

maybe millions. Newspapers and radio announce the route and the time when they ought to be along. Soon a crowd gathers, looking anxiously to see who is wearing the yellow jersey, which shows who is making the best time in the race.

There is little else to see. One moment the road is clear. Then official and advertising cars drive along. Suddenly the road is a blaze of colour, as the horde of cyclists passes by. As a show, it is all over in a few seconds, but the French are thrilled.

They have a game of bowls—called *boules* in the north

The French game of bowls—*boules*. In the background is the Ecole Militaire, Paris

and *pétanque* in the south. The bowls are made of metal, smaller than the wooden ones, but heavy. The game is not played on a trim piece of turf, but on any open space or even in a side road where the surface may be quite rough. This hazard, to the French, is one of the charms of the game.

The Frenchman loves to go shooting. He needs a licence, and the permission of the owner of a stretch of land. The sport appeals to the thrifty mind of the Frenchman: he gets exercise and excitement, and in addition he may bag a rabbit or a pheasant.

Or he may prefer to fish. Again, the joy of catching a fish which is good to eat is as important as the thrill of catching it.

Water sports such as swimming and boating are common. France has a wonderful system of rivers and canals, all joined up. From Calais or Boulogne, you could go by canoe or small boat right across France to the Mediterranean!

But a good many of the French are content to take their "sport" playing cards or dominoes at a café. Or they may prefer billiards which is played on a small table with no pockets.

Religion in France

France is classed as a Catholic country, although Church and State were separated early this century. When a couple wish to be married, they can arrange for the ceremony at a church. Yet legally that does not count—they must also have a civil ceremony at the office of the local mayor.

Not all the French are Catholics: there are Protestant minorities in Alsace and the central provinces. There is a Jewish community, and there are large numbers of Moslems from North Africa—some of whom are in France as students, but more as workers.

The parish priest is usually known as the *curé*. In towns he is one member of an organization, with a bishop and other authorities handy. In the village he is alone: often, in fact, in charge of two or three villages.

With the Act of Separation, the State took over the churches and *presbytères*, or vicarages, and is now responsible for keeping them in repair. The priest, however, is paid by his flock, which is not always rich. Most of his income comes from an annual collection from his parishioners.

He usually has a big garden, which he digs himself, and he may keep poultry or bees. Often he is a farmer's son, and so fits easily into village life. Many priests get trained in

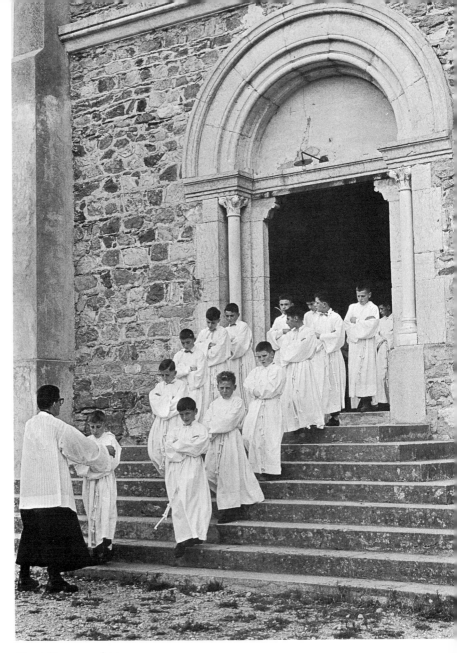

First Communion

first aid, for the doctor may be a distance away. He has no wife, of course, but some of the women of the parish help with the social side. He may earn a little extra by coaching children for examinations, for he is very well-educated by village standards.

On Thursdays he teaches the children their catechism, and prepares them for their first Communion, at the age of eleven or twelve. This is equivalent to being confirmed, and is a very important event in a French child's life.

The first Communion is a family affair, and relatives come from miles around. The girls wear long white dresses, with veils, and the boys have new suits—with a broad armband of ribbon—though in some parts of France they wear long white surplices, which the church lends to them for the occasion. Each is given a prayer-book and a candle, and they meet outside the *presbytère*. Some have come in by cart from outlying farms. They form a procession, and walk singing to the church, led by the curé.

After the long service, each party makes for home. There, a feast is waiting. Every room is crowded by relatives and friends. There is a special cake, and the children receive boxes of sugared almonds.

La Belle France

No country in the world can claim more famous sons than France. Napoleon Bonaparte was probably the greatest soldier in history, but France had very many others.

No matter in which direction you turn, you will find Frenchmen: in literature, Victor Hugo, Balzac, Molière, to name but three; in science, Joliot-Curie, discoverer of the power of radium; in medicine, Pasteur; in films, René Clair; in art, Picasso, Matisse and Degas; in architecture, Vauban, and Le Corbusier who spent most of his life in France, though he was born in Switzerland; in music, Gounod, Bizet, Debussy, Ravel and Saint-Saëns; in fashion, Christian Dior and a host of others—the list is endless.

We have done no more than glance at *la belle France*, as the French call it. The country is indeed beautiful, and its leisurely and cultured way of life has caught the imagination of countless generations.

Take a hundred intelligent people. Ask them to write down the name of the country they love best—the country in which they wish to live. Practically all will put down the name of their own country. But now ask them to make a second choice: which country do they like best *after* their own? I suspect that the vast majority will say "France!"

Index

95